with Dr Parikh

Dr Samir Parikh is a renowned psychiatrist, author and mentor. As the director of the Fortis National Mental Health Program and one of the leading experts in the country, Dr Parikh has played a significant role in creating awareness and shaping the narrative of positive mental health in India.

Twitter: @dr_samirparikh

About Fortis School Mental Health Program

The Fortis School Mental Health Program is a platform to promote psychosocial health and well-being amongst school-going children, as well as parents and teachers. This initiative is geared towards enhancing life skills and building resilience through interactive, fun-filled workshops in order to help students cope effectively with the challenges of everyday life.

Instagram: fortismentalhealth

Facebook: Fortis School Mental Health Program

Email: mentalhealth@fortishealthcare.com

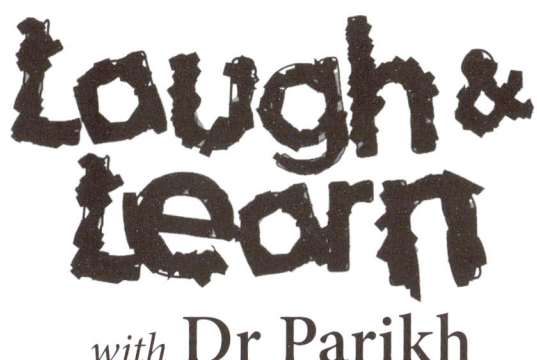

with **Dr Parikh**

Study and Exam Skills

Conceptualized by

Samir Parikh
Kamna Chhibber
Divya Jain
Mimansa Singh

RUPA

Published by
Rupa Publications India Pvt. Ltd 2019
7/16, Ansari Road, Daryaganj
New Delhi 110002

Sales centres:
Allahabad Bengaluru Chennai
Hyderabad Jaipur Kathmandu
Kolkata Mumbai

This is a work of fiction. Names, characters, places and incidents
are either the product of the author's imagination or are used
fictitiously and any resemblance to any actual person,
living or dead, events or locales is entirely coincidental.

ISBN: 978-93-5333-534-2

First impression 2019

10 9 8 7 6 5 4 3 2 1

The moral right of the author has been asserted.

Printed at Thomson Press India Ltd., Faridabad

Key Contributors

Tanushree Sangma

Aleena Ali

Ankit Chhabra

Craig Pinto

Farish Chander

Nikhil Bhati

mentalhealth@fortishealthcare.c

We've all been here. So, how high are your parents' expectations?

Breaks
are
important!

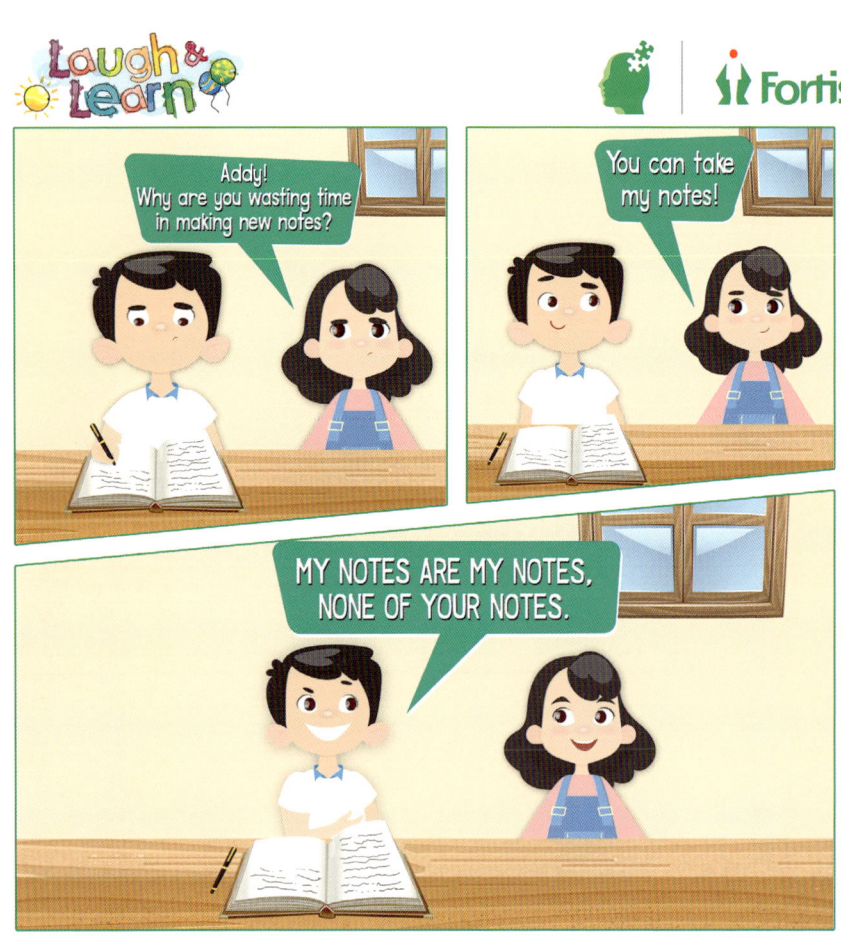

Make your own notes!

You know what, yesterday I tried the fun way of studying, i.e. with music!

Sounds cool! What did you learn?

I learned it was a bad idea to study with rap music and dance!

mentalhealth@fortishealthcare.cor

Avoid distraction,
maximize attention!

Switch off your phone to avoid distractions while studying.

Mnemonics make
learning fun!

Highlighting the important parts of the text always helps in doing a quick revision.

Test your concentration
every day.

Regular revision helps remember better.

mentalhealth@fortishealthcare.co

Focus on one thing
at a time.

mentalhealth@fortishealthcare.com

If you are sleepy at night, sleep!

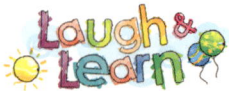

At night, during dinner time

Hey, Mom! Can you iron and keep my school uniform outside for tomorrow?

But it's a Sunday tomorrow.

Mom, relax... I'm creating 'THE' exam environment for a self-test tomorrow.

mentalhealth@fortishealthcare.com

Practise self-tests to reduce exam anxiety.

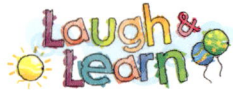

mentalhealth@fortishealthcare.cor

Grade your test to know where you stand.

mentalhealth@fortishealthcare.com

The coolest thing is to be yourself!

mentalhealth@fortishealthcare.c[o]

Self-evaluation of your studies helps boost both your and your parents' confidence levels.

mentalhealth@fortishealthcare.co

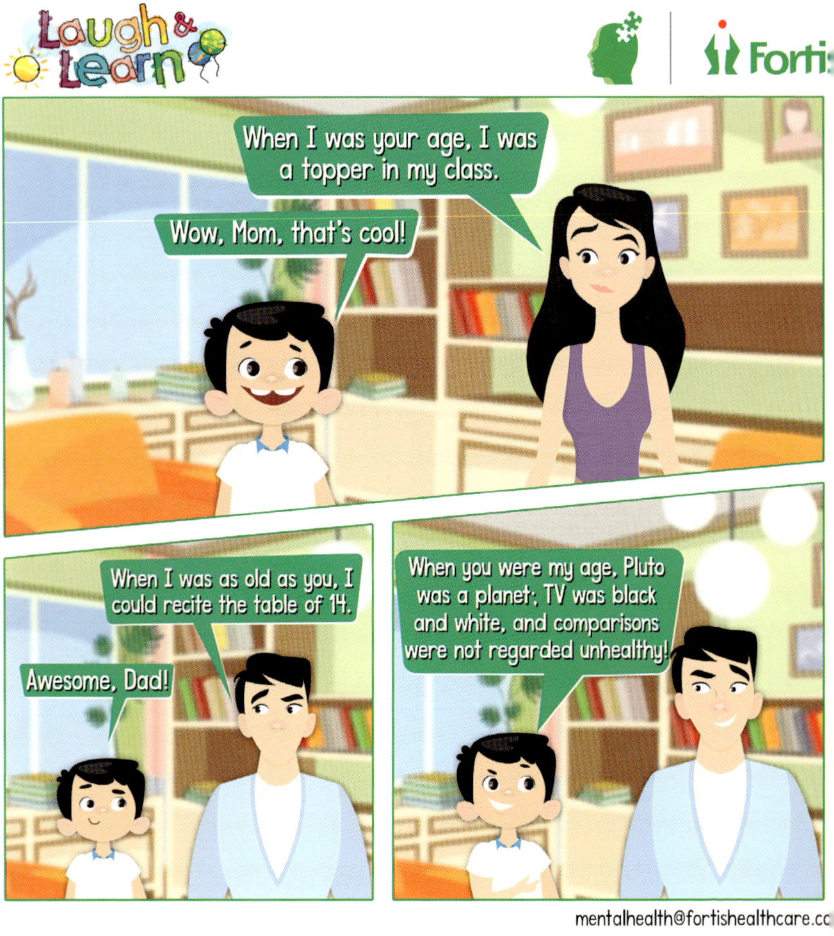

Avoid comparison.

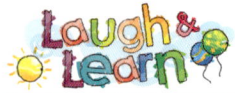

mentalhealth@fortishealthcare.c

Don't procrastinate.

Remember, one thing at a time!

Whether it's exam results or playing time, do not compare.

mentalhealth@fortishealthcare.com

Sleep in a bed at night.

mentalhealth@fortishealthcare.com

Be prepared for
what's important!

mentalhealth@fortishealthcare.co

A clear table makes you more able.

Eight hours of sleep
every night is a must.

Play a sport even during exam season to de-stress and improve performance.

mentalhealth@fortishealthcare.com

Sleep in your bed and study on your table.

Don't skip meals.

Parents, release the pressure!

mentalhealth@fortishealthcare.com

Parents, trust your child's efforts.

mentalhealth@fortishealthcare.com

Remember the
45-15 mantra!

It's an exam,
not a race!

mentalhealth@fortishealthcare.ca

Breaks are important. Take breaks!

mentalhealth@fortishealthcare.co

Comparisons don't help.

Make time to play outdoors!

mentalhealth@fortishealthcare.com

Don't stress. Relax.

mentalhealth@fortishealthcare.com

Support your children. Ask them how they are feeling.

Focus on your next exam.

mentalhealth@fortishealthcare.com

Mnemonics work,
memory pills don't!

Focus on **your** performance.

Remember the Energy
Mantra: sleep at night!

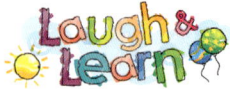

Take regular
outdoor breaks!

Parents, do not stress.

Avoid last-minute preparations.

Anayka's mom following her everywhere in study room, drawing room and balcony.

Don't you have to go to office?

No! I am on an Exam Prep Leave.

It's my exam not yours.

mentalhealth@fortishealthcare.com

Parents Relaxed
= Child relaxed

Anayka calling on Fortis Exam Helpline No. 8376804102

Helpline: Hello!
How can we help you?
How are you feeling today?

I am all fine, please talk to my mom, she is feeling stressed for my exams.

mentalhealth@fortishealthcare.com

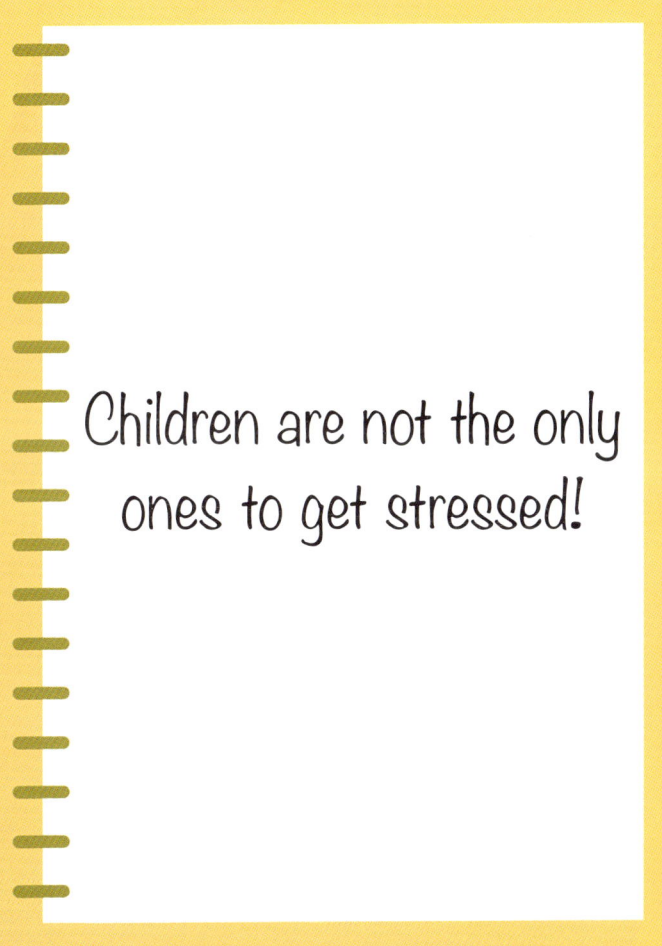

Children are not the only ones to get stressed!

mentalhealth@fortishealthcare.co

Use positive affirmations with your kids.

mentalhealth@fortishealthcare.co

Don't worry about answer sheets, stay focused on your own paper.

If you are set,
everything is set!

mentalhealth@fortishealthcare.co

Don't let the exams
stress you!

mentalhealth@fortishealthcare.co

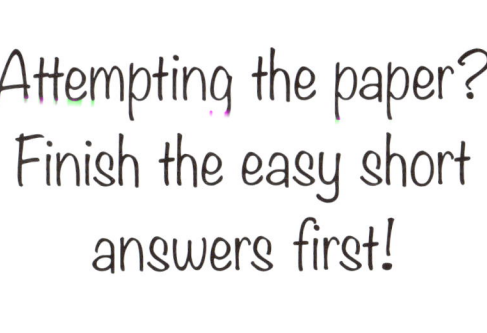

Attempting the paper?
Finish the easy short
answers first!

If you're ready for the exam, then there's no reason to panic.

All the best for
your exams!

DO IT YOURSELF

PRIORITY SQUARE

Unsure of where to start and what to do?
Let the priority square guide you.

1	**2**
Important and due soon	Important but not due soon
....	....
....	....
....	....
....	....

3	**4**
Not important but due soon	Not important and not due soon
....	....
....	....
....	....
....	....

SET YOUR GOALS

Short Term → Intermediate → Long Term

TAKE ONE STEP AT A TIME

MANAGING TIME

Always running late? Use this grid
to estimate your time correctly.

TASK	EXPECTED TIME	COMPLETED TIME

BREAKS: To Do and NOT To Do

Breaks are a crucial part of the 45-15 rule. Here are some dos and dont's for a quick break.

TO DO	NOT TO DO
Leave your study room	Watch television
Drink plenty of water	Scroll social media
Eat a healthy snack	Play video games
Talk to your family	Read
Call your friends	Drink tea, coffee or colas
Listen to music	Surf the internet
Wash your face	Text on the phone
Relax	Worry

CONCENTRATION DRILL I

Take a newspaper article. Cancel all the letter 'e's that you come across in the article without making any mistakes. Do this once a day, and try to better your time with every attempt.

CONCENTRATION DRILL II

Listen to a piece of instrumental music (at least three or four instruments playing). Follow the sound of any one instrument while tuning out all the others. Do this for five minutes before each study session to zone-in.

MNEMONICS

Have fun with Mnemonics. Write down
your favourite Mnemonics here!

....

....

....

....

....

....

....

....

....

....

....

....

....

SELF-EVALUATION GRID

You don't need your parents or teachers to tell you to study. Set your own expectations and score yourself from 1–5.

1	2	3	4	5

DATE	EFFORT SCORE

REVISION ROUTINE

DID YOU KNOW?

People forget most of what they learn within one week. Follow this revision routine to race ahead of the human forgetting curve.

| Day 1 | Day 2 | Day 7 | Day 15 | Day 30 |

MOCK TEST CHECKLIST

✓   Prepare your own question paper

✓   Wear your school uniform

✓   Create an exam-like environment

✓   Attempt the paper within the fixed time

✓   Check your answers with a red pen

✓   Give yourself your final marks

THE HIGH FIVE OF EXAM TIME

1. Sleep for eight hours every night

2. Play outdoors every day

3. Talk to friends and family

4. Take regular breaks

5. Have fun

REACH OUT

If you're stressed, you don't have to deal with it
all on your own. Call us on our 24x7
helpline number **+918376804102**.

STAY TUNED!
WE WILL BE
BACK SOON WITH
OUR NEXT BOOK
IN THE SERIES...

NOTES

NOTES

....
....
....
....
....
....
....
....
....
....
....
....
....

NOTES

NOTES

NOTES

....
....
....
....
....
....
....
....
....
....
....
....
....
....

NOTES